Pandas

Children Book of Fun Facts & Amazing Photos on Animals in Nature - A Wonderful Pandas Book for Kids aged 3-7

By

Ina Felix

Ina Felix

Copyright © 2015 by Ina Felix

All rights reserved. No part of this book may be used or reproduced in any manner whatsoever without the express written permission of the publisher except for the use of brief quotations in a book review. Image Credits: Royalty free images reproduced under license from various stock image repositories. Under a creative commons licenses.

Hi! I am a panda.

Ina Felix

Here are some cool things about me.

I belong to the bear family.

I am a mammal.

I love climbing trees.

I love to cuddle.

I have a good sense of smell.

I am from China and I live in the forest.

I am born hairless and I am only 5 feet long.

My favorite foods are bamboos, grasses, some insects, and fruits.

I am a loner but I love making friends with other animals.

I spend my day eating, sleeping, and playing whenever I feel like it.

I have an awesome mom that takes good care of me.

I may look like I'm quiet but I roar, growl, and honk.

I am super cute and very playful!

I wear a black and white shirt and shorts every day.

I hide in caves or in hollow trees when it gets cold.

I'm shy and one of a kind in the world!

I have friends name tigress, monkey, crane, and snake.

I love the water! I love to swim in it and drink lots of it as well so I can be healthy and strong.

I hope you had fun learning about my family.

Thank you.

Made in the USA
Columbia, SC
09 December 2018